BOOK ANALYSIS

Written by Hudson Cleveland

No Country for Old Men

BY CORMAC MCCARTHY

CORMAC MCCARTHY   9

NO COUNTRY FOR OLD MEN   13

SUMMARY   17

Sheriff Bell's thoughts
Llewelyn Moss at the crime scene
Chigurh on the move
Looking for Llewelyn Moss
Leaving the motel, and trouble at the Hotel Eagle
Finding Moss
Moss and Chigurh discuss terms
Finding Moss
The End Game
Bell's final thoughts

CHARACTER STUDY   29

Sheriff Ed Tom Bell
Llewelyn Moss
Anton Chigurh
Carla Jean
Carson Wells
Loretta Bell
Uncle Ellis
The hitchhiker

ANALYSIS   37

Punctuation and McCarthy's writing style
Chance, fate, luck
Subversion of the mystery/thriller/crime genre

FURTHER REFLECTION   47

FURTHER READING   53

CORMAC MCCARTHY

AMERICAN NOVELIST

- **Born in Providence, Rhode Island in 1933.**
- **Notable works:**
  - *Blood Meridian or the Evening Redness in the West* (1985), novel
  - *Border Trilogy (1992-1998)*, series of novels
  - *The Road* (2006), novel

Cormac McCarthy is often cited as one of America's most important contemporary writers, particularly for his 1985 novel *Blood Meridian*. While he had been pursuing writing as a career as early as the 1960s (his first novel, *The Orchard Keeper*, was published in 1965), he did not start to garner widespread acclaim and commercial success until the publication of his later works, including *Blood Meridian* and especially his *Border Trilogy*, starting with *All the Pretty Horses* (1992).

McCarthy's writing is known for two primary reasons: his depictions of the American South, and his writing style. In particular, McCarthy has attracted praise for his use of dialect in his novels focusing on the South, while his writing style is noted for stripping away as many commas, apostrophes and punctuation marks as he can, even removing quotation marks for dialogue.

NO COUNTRY FOR OLD MEN

A WORLD THAT OLDER MEN ONCE UNDERSTOOD FALLS TO CHAOTIC VIOLENCE

- **Genre:** novel
- **Reference edition:** McCarthy, C. (2010) *No Country for Old Men*. London: Picador.
- **1ˢᵗ edition:** 2005
- **Themes:** crime, the rise of chaos, family, fate and chance, senseless violence, self-sufficiency, rural America

It is 1980 in rural Texas. Local county sheriff Ed Tom Bell finds himself in an increasingly violent world that he understands less and less every day. Llewelyn Moss, a Vietnam veteran and a welder by trade, stumbles across the aftermath of a drug-deal gone bad while out hunting. Instead of reporting the incident, he decides to take the briefcase full of money he finds there and run off with it. This brings him to the attention not only of Sheriff Bell, but also of two rival cartels and the murderous, psychopathic Anton Chigurh. Moss is forced to flee through all of Texas and Mexico to avoid the forces after him, including the Sheriff, who is trying to make sure Moss survives the situation he has gotten himself into, and Chigurh, who will stop at nothing, even being given the money, to kill Moss.

SUMMARY

SHERIFF BELL'S THOUGHTS

Sheriff Ed Tom Bell reflects on the execution of a young man that he once witnessed. Similar reflections occur at the beginning of every subsequent chapter. Following this, a man in custody named Anton Chigurh kills the Deputy who arrested him and flees from his office.

LLEWELYN MOSS AT THE CRIME SCENE

Hiking away after a missed shot that scattered the antelopes he was hunting, Llewelyn Moss comes across three bullet-ridden vehicles surrounded by several dead men. One, still alive but barely, begs for water. Moss finds another dead man some distance away, as well as a briefcase containing several million dollars. He is "scared in a way he [doesn't] even understand" (p. 17).

Moss takes the money and returns home to his trailer, where he talks briefly and obliquely to his wife, Carla Jean, about what occurred. At 1:06 the following morning he wakes and contemplates the fortune he has taken, then takes a gallon of water to the crime scene, where he discovers that the dying man has been killed. There follows a drawn-out gunfight along a nearby river by which Moss attempts, and finally does manage, to escape.

CHIGURH ON THE MOVE

The police begin moving in reaction to Chigurh's murderous escape. Meanwhile, Moss finally gets home to his trailer, where he tells Carla Jean to skip town.

Chigurh reaches a gas station. He gets into a strange discussion with the proprietor, which ends with Chigurh making him call a coin toss. The threat of fatal violence hangs over the scene, but the man calls it correctly and Chigurh leaves. Later that evening, he meets with two men and goes with them to Moss' abandoned truck and then to the crime scene, where he kills them and acquires a receiver that tracks the briefcase of money.

LOOKING FOR LLEWELYN MOSS

Moss parts company with Carla Jean, leaving her on a bus to her grandmother's. Sheriff Bell is called to a crime scene, along with a deputy named Wendell: the scene of both the original crime and the more recent incidents that took place nearby. Later, Bell and another deputy, Torbert, discuss the gruesome deaths, where Bell reflects, "I aint sure we've seen these people before. Their kind. I dont know what to do about em even" (p. 79).

Chigurh has found Moss' abandoned trailer and ransacks it. He begins making inquiries in the surrounding area regarding Moss' whereabouts. Moss, meanwhile, is hiding in another town. He gets a motel room, patches himself up and gathers supplies, including a shotgun, quickly realising that despite Carla Jean telling him not to hurt anyone, "he knew that he was probably going to have to kill somebody" (p. 87). He hides the briefcase of money deep in his motel room's air duct.

LEAVING THE MOTEL, AND TROUBLE AT THE HOTEL EAGLE

Bell and his deputies follow the trail Chigurh and Moss leave behind. DEA agent McIntyre, who has been sent to help Bell investigate, arrives via helicopter.

The main plot is briefly interrupted by a vignette of Chigurh taking a shot at a bird with a silenced pistol. This is one of many instances depicting his capacity for random acts of cruelty – though his shot misses.

Moss purchases a second room at the same motel, deducing that someone has broken into the first one. He fishes the briefcase from the second room's air duct, then leaves the motel.

Chigurh arrives at the motel. A group of men from one of the involved gangs have taken over Moss' first room. Chigurh kills them, finds the drag marks left in the air duct by the briefcase, cleans himself quietly of blood, and leaves.

Moss has taken a cab to another city, where he takes a room at the Hotel Eagle. He inspects his briefcase of money, and finds the transponder inside. Setting it in the bedroom drawer, he goes and pays the clerk to call him if anyone suspicious walks into the hotel.

Moss wakes up of his own accord, thinking someone could be coming. He catches Chigurh walking into his room. Moss does not kill him, instead choosing to disarm him and run. Chigurh pulls out his silenced pistol and a shootout follows through the hotel lobby and outside, with other parties joining in the firefight. Moss escapes, bleeding heavily, and manages to hide the briefcase and cross the U.S.-Mexico border to get help at the Piedras Negras Hospital before passing out. Chigurh himself has a leg wound, but kills all the parties who had joined in the shootout. Chigurh executes the last man left alive after ordering him to look Chigurh in the eye.

FINDING MOSS

Bell meets Carla Jean, now staying with her grandmother. Bell attempts to gather information on Moss from her at the Sunshine Café. She does not let any key information slip, even saying that she would die before snitching on Moss. As readers, we learn here that Moss was a soldier in the Vietnam War (1955-1975).

Bell is called to the crime scene at the Hotel Eagle late at night. When he returns home, he has a brief discussion with his wife about Moss, for whom he appears to have genuine sympathy and worry.

A man named Wells discusses Chigurh with someone who seems to be a high-ranking cartel officer. The two characterise Chigurh as an actual psychopath, unable to be controlled and even, according to the officer, "invincible" (p. 140).

Wells is waiting by Moss' side when he wakes at the hospital. He tells Moss as explicitly as he can how dangerous a man Chigurh is – outlining how Carla Jean is in danger also, and that even if Moss kills Chigurh there will be an endless number of other men sent after him until the money is recovered – and how he, Wells, is the only one who can help at this point. Moss sees why Wells would help him: he would "rather deal with [Moss] than this sugar guy" (p. 155). He gives Moss his phone number and leaves, expecting him to call later even if Moss thinks he will not.

MOSS AND CHIGURH DISCUSS TERMS

Chigurh meticulously cleans his leg wound and spends five days recovering at a motel. He tracks the transponder, and then finds and corners Wells at the Hotel Eagle. Wells offers to pay him off, but Chigurh says that his wound changed him, "Changed [his] perspective. [He's] moved on in a way" (p. 173). Chigurh explains the reason he was under arrest at the beginning of the novel: killing someone with whom he provoked a fight. Wells calls him "goddamned crazy" (p. 175). Chigurh keeps talking to him about their positions, for so long that Wells begins commanding him to get it over with (i.e. kill him). Chigurh finally does.

Moss calls Carla Jean. He tells her that he might have found someone who can help them (Wells). He calls Wells, but Chigurh answers. Chigurh tells him that unless they meet, Carla Jean will be "accountable. Same as you [Moss]" (p. 184).

Moss crosses the U.S.-Mexico border back into Texas. Meanwhile, Sheriff Bell has arrived at the second crime scene at the Hotel Eagle: Wells' murder.

FINDING MOSS

Chigurh kills the ranking man who had hired Wells. Carla Jean flees to El Paso with her grandmother, and Chigurh searches the grandmother's house shortly after.

Moss retrieves the briefcase from where he hid it, then pays a cab driver to take him to San Antonio. He buys a gun and a car. While driving out of the city, he picks up a girl hitchhiking. He makes her drive so that he can rest, his wounds still hurting him.

Carla Jean calls Sheriff Bell from El Paso. She has decided to tell Bell where Moss last called from. We are then shown a small scene at the end of the chapter, showing that cartel members have wiretapped Bell's home phone and have now caught on to Moss' trail.

Moss and the hitchhiking girl have several conversations about one another, omitting key details, as they head west toward El Paso (for Moss) and California (for her), stopping at a diner, truck stop and finally at a motel in Van Horn for the night.

THE END GAME

Bell makes it to Van Horn, only to find that Moss and the girl have been killed overnight. Bell goes to El Paso to tell Carla Jean of Moss' death in person.

Chigurh meets with the cartel leader for whom the briefcase of money was originally meant. He gives him the money instead of keeping it for himself, deciding to strike up a business relationship.

After Carla Jean attends her mother's funeral, she finds Chigurh waiting for her at home. He has come to fulfil his earlier promise to kill her, since Moss decided against giving the money to Chigurh in order to end the situation. He decides, like with the gas station proprietor from near the beginning of the novel, to decide her fate with a coin toss, which she calls incorrectly. He calls it bad luck. After a discussion, almost a sermon, like he had with Wells, he shoots her.

Chigurh, in an ironic twist, gets in a severe car accident. He survives with some broken bones and pays off bystanders to say they did not see him there before leaving the scene.

BELL'S FINAL THOUGHTS

Bell has decided to retire soon. He goes to his uncle Ellis' home and talks for a long time with him – in a way, their discussion synthesises all the reflections we read from Bell at the start of each chapter. Bell confesses to Ellis that the act for which he received a Bronze Star in World War II (1939-1945) was followed by abandoning his squadron to a German grenade volley. He thought the guilt would go away, but when it did not he "thought that maybe [he] could make up for it" (p. 278). This has been what he has tried to do during his long tenure as sheriff.

Bell talks to the bystanders that Chigurh paid off after getting a call about Carla Jean's murder. From one of them he finally manages to get a profile, albeit a vague one, on Chigurh. But we never see Chigurh captured or killed, if he ever is. The denouement shows Sheriff Bell winding into retirement, and the novel ends with a last reflection of his: a dream he had of his father after he died.

CHARACTER STUDY

SHERIFF ED TOM BELL

Ed Tom Bell is the sheriff of Terrell County, Texas. He is reaching an older age, and finds it difficult to apply his older and more coherent moral systems to what he sees as an increasingly chaotic and violent world. While he attempts to protect Llewelyn Moss and his wife Carla Jean, both are ultimately killed, and the failure of Bell's values to subdue the forces which killed them leads him to retire come the novel's end.

While Llewelyn Moss seems to be the protagonist of the novel, since the story revolves around the act of him taking the money, Sheriff Bell fits the role more aptly. His perspective and reflections are core to the novel's themes, coming as they do at the beginning of every chapter, and he acts in a sense as the detective in a detective-fiction that unfolds in tandem with his discoveries.

Bell is more or less disregarded by the other main characters, Moss and Chigurh. Bell in fact reflects that "probably the only reason [he is] even still alive is that they have no respect for [him]" (p. 217), further evidence of the way the world he knew (the country of old men, as the title says) is slipping into depravity, violence and chaos that he cannot even begin to control.

Though it is not revealed until near the end of the novel, Bell has spent his time as sheriff attempting to work away the guilt he had accrued after abandoning his fellow soldiers to a German grenade volley in World War II.

LLEWELYN MOSS

Llewelyn Moss catalyses the rest of the story when he takes a large sum of money from the scene of a drug-deal gone bad, all parties in it dead or dying. Evidently a risk-taker based on this decision, we see his experience as a soldier in Vietnam guide him through several gunfights and get him out of puzzle-like situations.

Moss thinks himself completely self-sufficient. Even as he goes on the run from the cartels, Chigurh and Sheriff Bell, he still tries to help his wife Carla Jean flee town and survive. Indeed, the reason he took the money was so that the two could live in comfort. He declines the assistance of Wells (until it is too late) and Bell, but that very focus on his own strength and ability comes to be his downfall.

Moss acts as a foil to Bell in terms of what they took away from their military experiences. While World War II is acknowledged as the greatest and bloodiest conflict in modern history, its goals at least were clear: to halt the expansion of the Axis powers. Vietnam, however, has for a long time been regarded as costly, ineffective and questionable in terms of desired outcomes. Thus, while Bell sees a violent but structured world turn more violent and less structured, his relied-upon systems failing him, Moss recognises the chaos and depravity of it and relies on his own self, something which had not failed him yet. Of course, his sudden death, which does not even happen on-page, proves this system to be just as tenuous as Bell's: he has no safety net to fall back on in the event of unforeseen circumstances, circumstances which immediately overpower his knowledge, wit and strength.

ANTON CHIGURH

Anton Chigurh embodies the very chaos and violence that Sheriff Bell cannot come to understand. He has a predilection for random acts of cruelty and intimidation, and has no qualms about killing anyone inconvenient to him. His status in the novel is practically elemental: despite his monologues it is difficult to gauge what exactly he stands for, particularly since he kills those helping him track Moss at the beginning of the novel, kills the man who hired Wells, kills Carla Jean even after Moss' death and strikes up a business relationship with the intended recipient of the briefcase of money even after his strange, off-putting philosophical musings.

Chigurh's weapon of choice is a cattle gun, a killing device which utilises air pressure to launch a metal bolt into and back out of the brain. Chigurh uses this also to blow the locks off of doors. The cattle gun exhibits just how little he thinks of human life: any death by it more or less parallels that death to the distant and desensitised killings of animals in a slaughterhouse. This quick, controlled means of murder also mirrors Chigurh's clinical and detached nature.

Chigurh's philosophy seems to revolve, to a degree, around the role of chance and fate, even though he, like Sheriff Bell and Moss, recognises the chaotic nature of the world he lives in. He leaves two people's lives down to a coin toss, saying that "[he] got [there] the same way the coin did" (p. 258). Yet he also exhibits strains of the same self-sufficiency that Moss carries, as he touches on in his conversation with Wells.

All in all, Chigurh is a psychopathic and enigmatic figure. The philosophical aspects of his character are both limited in scope and inexplicable by nature: neither Moss, Wells, Carla Jean nor several unnamed characters he crosses paths with seem to fully understand his motives.

CARLA JEAN

Moss' wife, whom he shuts out of all conversation regarding the money for her own safety. Her grandmother has cancer, and happens to die shortly after Moss is murdered. When Chigurh comes to kill her, he describes it as such: "None of this was your fault. [...] You didn't do anything. It was bad luck" (p. 257), summing up the inevitability of Moss' decision having a ripple effect, even though it was seemingly made in a vacuum and in spite of his supposed self-sufficiency.

CARSON WELLS

A Vietnam veteran like Moss, Wells is a hitman sent to recover the money. He is rigorous in his work, and has a strong memory for numbers and details. He attempts to strike a deal with Moss, favouring working with him over Chigurh, but dies by Chigurh's hand before Moss agrees. Wells makes it clear to Moss that his attempts to cover his tracks were completely unsuccessful, undermining Moss' confidence in his self-sufficiency.

LORETTA BELL

Sheriff Bell's wife. She partly grounds Bell's faith in the older way of the world, but eventually is not enough to do so: he still retires.

UNCLE ELLIS

Bell's uncle, and a retired sheriff. Ellis, one of the 'old men' the title evokes, has shut himself away from the world on the family homestead, rarely seeing visitors. Ellis is the first person in Bell's inner circle to whom Bell confides his World War II guilt.

THE HITCHHIKER

A nameless young woman traveling to California that Moss picks up. Like Carla Jean, she embodies someone with 'bad luck', simply getting caught in the crossfire of a situation they were not willing participants in. She and Moss have several long conversations about escaping problems and the past.

ANALYSIS

PUNCTUATION AND MCCARTHY'S WRITING STYLE

Perhaps the most immediately noticeable aspect of *No Country for Old Men* is Cormac McCarthy's characteristic style of writing: dropping commas, colons and even apostrophes as frequently as coherence will allow, and even leaving behind the idea of quotation marks entirely.

The absence of quotation marks in particular is striking for a novel so laden with dialogue. In some ways, it even reads more like a film script than a book (perhaps part of the reason for the widespread acclaim of the Coen Brothers' film adaptation of the same name [2007]).

The effects of this writing style are multiple. The most evident one is that readers are not given any 'fluff' material, any description that does not directly pertain to the action or dialogue on the page, which works in the favour of a novel so heavily reliant on high-stakes action and dialogue to drive its story forward. There are no distractions taking attention away from the bluntly-pictured scenes of brutality.

Because McCarthy eschews the use of commas where he can, and he frequently employs instead what is known as a polysyndeton: that is, repeated usage of conjunctions, for example, "He turned **and** leaned against the fence **and** raised the small cheap camera he carried **and** took a picture of nothing in particular **and** lowered the camera again" (p. 166; emphasis added). A technique reminiscent of another American author, Ernest Hemingway (1899-1961), the polysyndeton, coupled with McCarthy's stripping down of punctuation, gives the words on the page a sort of numb flow, where so much happens but the action feels distant, as if the narrator were describing things after a sort of trauma. Which, given the content of *No Country for Old Men* (as well as many of McCarthy's other works), seems fitting: Bell's inability to understand the senseless violence of his times gels with that matter-of-fact writing style.

In the dialogue, we are given few indicators of emotion, or even of the current speaker (though for the latter, McCarthy structures conversations and dialects in such a way as to rarely, if ever, engender confusion). This can create a 'numb flow' similar to that mentioned in the prior paragraph, and many of the characters – in particular Bell, Moss and especially Chigurh – actually seem to think in this manner. However, it also leaves open the imposition of the reader's interpretations of the text, the film adaptation showing just how certain 'dry dialogue' scenes could be rendered. In addition, when emotions do become overt – for instance, when Bell informs Carla Jean of Moss' death, when Chigurh visits Carla Jean or when Chigurh discourses with Wells before killing him – they have the ability to hit the reader all the harder due to the distanced style of the dialogue bookending those moments.

CHANCE, FATE, LUCK

A common feature of the 'American myth' is an individual who triumphs over the odds, beats 'fated' outcomes, and bounces back from bouts of bad luck. *No Country for Old Men* chops this comforting idea into pieces. Moss has the good fortune to stumble upon the botched drug-deal and makes off with the money, but this chance encounter leads ultimately to his death. Despite his status as the main character, this death also comes without warning, and well before the end of the book. Sheriff Bell has his faith in a teleological outcome – that the 'good guys' will win out over the 'bad guys' – shattered by the violence thrust at random upon his county, as well as by the unsolved nature of the crimes he tracks. He yearns for the recognisable order of years gone by, but that order remains ineluctable at the time of the novel's end, and he gives up, going into retirement. Chigurh becomes the most successful of the trio, obtaining the money and wiping out anyone standing in his way. Even his clean getaway, however, is tarnished when he is t-boned at an intersection: something entirely not his fault, but which he happened to run into anyway. He still gets away, but severely injured.

Other examples of a failed American faith in one's luck (or, simply, bad luck) abound in the novel, but Chigurh's monologues summarise the theme succinctly, if enigmatically. Three of the monologues can be singled out as the most significant: the first is the coin toss scene with the gas station proprietor; the second, his meeting with Carson Wells; the third, his meeting with Carla Jean.

These conversations exhibit not only Chigurh's unstated belief in his position outside of any understandable centring force (he escapes the law, kills people with little provocation, kills cartel members on multiple sides and even has little concern for his own pain), but his unblinking acceptance of incalculable and unforeseen circumstances. This is not to say that the novel rejects any notion of autonomy, but that that autonomy comes only after the occurrence of said unforeseen circumstances: in the form of a decision. The primary example of such a decision is Moss deciding to take the money at the beginning of the novel. However, it is also worth noting that Chigurh has become so detached from any sense of morality that making the easiest and most self-serving decision – killing those in his way – has become practically second nature to him ("Because I'm in charge of who is coming and who is not" [p. 251]). When faced with the gas station proprietor, Wells, and Carla Jean, he seems to scorn the way that they find it difficult or impossible to accept the circumstances that landed them with Chigurh, and the fact that they are unable to recognise their ordained place, like the coins he flips, in the chaos of the world: "Yes you did [bet something on the coin toss]. You've been putting it up your whole life. You just didn't know it" (p. 56).

Thus, the main commentary on chance and fate is that one cannot (always or fully) control the circumstances which bring one to a junction (Carla Jean: "The coin didn't have no say. It was just you." Chigurh: "Perhaps. But look at it my way. I got here the same way the coin did. [...] For things at a common destination there is a common path" [p. 258-259]), but once one arrives at that junction, you have one method of control: choice, even the simple choice of calling heads or tails on a coin toss.

SUBVERSION OF THE MYSTERY/ THRILLER/CRIME GENRE

No Country for Old Men does indeed fall under the categories of mystery, thriller and crime, but at several turns it subverts the expectations for those genres.

For the crime (or detective) genre, a suitable archetype to think of is the Sherlock Holmes stories and novels (1887-1927) by British author Sir Arthur Conan Doyle (1859-1930). The general arc of these stories is being introduced to the aftermath of a crime, then the detective (in Doyle's case, Sherlock Holmes; in McCarthy's case, Sheriff Bell) piecing together what happened from various clues and apprehending the likely suspect. Instead, in *No Country for Old Men*, Sheriff Bell follows the crime in real time, and rather than there being any resolution or criminals apprehended, the man Bell wanted to protect (Moss) is killed and the amoral criminal he had been chasing (Chigurh) gets away.

Similarly, *No Country for Old Men* subverts the conventions of the thriller or action genre. In most of these, a protagonist will be hyped up to have a final battle or shootout with the antagonist. But, despite the suspense constantly increasing between Moss and Chigurh, with their initial shootout and Moss essentially declaring war by saying he would "make [Chigurh] a special project of [his]" (p. 185), Moss dies without ever again encountering Chigurh.

What is the purpose of these subversions? As with any subversion of genre tropes, a primary goal might be to point out the limitations, or perhaps unrealistic patterns, of the popularly expected tropes. Another is that if the audience expects one thing to occur based on what they have seen in past iterations of the genre, but a new and wholly unexpected event occurs, the novelty of the experience lends itself to the entertainment value of the novel. A final reading would be that these subversions line up perfectly with the previously-discussed themes of the novel: random chance, the inability of the individual (be it Moss or Sheriff Bell) to stand up to chaotic forces, and the inability of old relied-upon patterns or tropes to explain new developments in the world.

FURTHER REFLECTION

SOME QUESTIONS TO THINK ABOUT...

- Chigurh's motives are difficult to pin down – partway through the novel, he even says that the wound he sustained in the gunfight with Moss changed him, but the way it changed him is never made clear – but what are some potential interpretations to be had, given his actions and his brief monologues?
- Are Sheriff Bell's notions of the increasing unintelligibility of the violence in his home state applicable to the world at large? If so, in what capacity? What are some examples?
- What does the novel have to say about fate, luck and chance?
- Llewelyn Moss prides himself on his self-sufficiency and his ability to care for not only himself but those he holds dear (namely, Carla Jean). How does his failed attempt at self-sufficiency contrast with Chigurh's own?

- The conclusion of Chigurh's monologue to the gas station proprietor is as follows:

  > "Anything can be an instrument. [...] Well, you say. It's just a coin. For instance. Nothing special there. What could that be an instrument of? You see the problem. To separate the act from the thing. As if the parts of some moment in history might be interchangeable with the parts of some other moment. Well, it's just a coin. Yes. That's true. Is it?" (p. 57).

  How does this statement figure in with characters who seem to do little in the story (DEA agent McIntyre, Deputy Wendell, even the gas station proprietor)?

- "Dope." "They sell that shit to schoolkids." "It's worse than that." "How's that?" "Schoolkids buy it" (p. 194). In the late 1970s and leading into the 1980s (the novel being set in 1980), the U.S. 'War on Drugs' began and cartelisation of drug trafficking peaked. How well does *No Country for Old Men* depict the numerous people and industries (acting directly in it, or simply implicated indirectly, as the schoolkids might be) that formed the supply and the demand, as well as the conflict, of this complex system?

- Most popular works which feature violence are criticised for the 'gratuitousness' of this violence. To what end could it be said that McCarthy utilises extreme violence in *No Country for Old Men*? Is it gratuitous, or does it serve a greater thematic purpose?
- Two of the novel's main characters, Sheriff Bell and Llewelyn Moss, are war veterans. What commentary does *No Country for Old Men* provide on what soldiers bring back home from armed conflicts?
- Sheriff Bell confesses his wartime guilt, which only he knew; Chigurh says that Moss is accountable for his actions and that if he plays it wrong Carla Jean will be accountable as well; Chigurh, though, appears by the novel's end to get away with all the heinous and brutal acts he committed over the course of the narrative with little more than broken bones, which he ignores. Bearing this in mind, how does *No Country for Old Men* treat themes of responsibility?

We want to hear from you!
Leave a comment on your online library
and share your favourite books on social media!

FURTHER READING

REFERENCE EDITION

- McCarthy, C. (2010) *No Country for Old Men*. London: Picador.

ADAPTATIONS

- *No Country for Old Men*. (2007) [Film]. Joel and Ethan Coen. Dir. USA: Miramax, Paramount.

MORE FROM BRIGHTSUMMARIES.COM

- Reading guide – *The Road* by Cormac McCarthy.

www.brightsummaries.com

Ebook EAN: 9782808015998

Paperback EAN: 9782808016001

Legal Deposit: D/2018/12603/560

Cover: © Primento

Digital conception by Primento, the digital partner of publishers.